William Buckley

Dianne Irving

Contents

Back in Time

I'm Aidan and this is my cool time machine! It takes me back in time. I get to see lots of interesting things from the past, but no one can see me.

When it's time to leave, the machine makes a beeping sound that only I can hear.

I never know where my time machine is going to take me until I get there. I wonder where it will take me today …

William Buckley

It is the year 1835. From my time machine, I see a group of people sitting around a fire. There is a man talking to the group about his life.

I wonder who he is … I listen carefully.

The man's name is William Buckley. I find out he was born in England. He was a bricklayer's apprentice but he didn't like it. So he ran away and became a soldier.

William Buckley was very tall – about 198 centimetres!

One day, William was found carrying some stolen cloth. He said he didn't know it was stolen, but he was found guilty. He was sentenced to be **transported** to Australia.

Transportation

Many people found guilty of a crime in England were sentenced to be transported. That means they were sent to live as prisoners in another country, at a **penal settlement**. This was a place where **convicts** lived and worked.

Convicts working at a penal settlement.

Sullivan Bay, 1803

In 1803, William came to Port Phillip Bay on the *Calcutta*, with about 300 other prisoners. A new penal settlement was going to be set up at Sullivan Bay.

Sullivan Bay

The penal settlement at Sullivan Bay was the first **European** settlement in Victoria. But the settlement did not do well – there was not enough fresh water available and the land was not good for crop growing.

Escape

After about three months at the penal settlement, William decided to escape with two other convicts. They headed to the beach and found shellfish to eat, but after a few weeks they were very hungry and thirsty.

The two other convicts decided to return to the penal settlement at Sullivan Bay, but William wanted to keep going. He wanted to reach Sydney. He thought Sydney was not far away!

William walked around most of Port Phillip Bay looking for food, water and shelter. His clothes were in rags, his shoes were worn out and he was not healthy. So he decided to head back to the penal settlement at Sullivan Bay.

European Settlers

When William Buckley was transported to Australia, the only area to have European **settlers** was New South Wales.

The First Meeting

Later that day, I found out that William hadn't made it back to the penal settlement at Sullivan Bay. One day while he was still walking, he saw a mound of dirt. A spear was sticking out of the ground nearby. He was tired, so he used the spear as a walking stick.

Van Diemen's Land

Even if William had made it back to the penal settlement, there would have been nobody there. Everyone had left and gone to settle in Van Diemen's Land, which is now called Tasmania.

A group of Aboriginal women saw William with the spear and they took him back to their group. William was scared. But when they gave him food and water, and performed a corroboree in his honour, he knew they were his friends.

A Corroboree

A corroboree is an Aboriginal ceremony where there is singing and dancing. The word "corroboree" was used by European settlers. It comes from the Aboriginal word "caribberie".

The Aboriginal people thought William was an Aboriginal man who had died and come back to life. The man was buried in the mound William had seen. They called William "Murrangurk" after the man who had died.

Aboriginal Beliefs

Aboriginal people believed that sometimes when one of their people died, they would return to the Earth as a white person.

Part of the Tribe

William became part of the Wathaurong tribe. He learned their **customs** and their language, and lived with them for more than 30 years.

Everyone worked together and shared the food they caught. Even young children provided food by digging for roots. The **tribe** would move from place to place to find food and water.

William learned to hunt kangaroos using a spear. He also used his spear to catch eels. He learned to skin animals using mussel shells.

His tribe gave him a rug made of animal furs. He wore this and used it to sleep on. Aboriginal people slept on the ground. They made huts using branches and bark.

Buckley Falls

There are falls on the Barwon River called Buckley Falls. They were named after William Buckley.

As part of the Wathaurong tribe, William witnessed Aboriginal burial ceremonies. Sometimes the person was buried in the ground and their spears were put in the ground nearby.

Sometimes a shelf was made high in the trees. The person was put on the shelf facing the Sun, and then covered with bark and branches.

An Aboriginal burial platform

The Wathaurong tribe often performed corroborees. The men and women painted their bodies with clay. They would sing and dance.

Sometimes they visited other tribes. Sometimes there was fighting between the tribes.

Aboriginal men performing a corroboree

I loved listening to William tell about his life with the Wathaurong people. He had lived with them for a long time. It was interesting to listen to how Aboriginal people had lived before the European settlement of Australia.

Discovery Trail

In Victoria, there is a "William Buckley Discovery Trail", which has signs at 19 of the places he is believed to have travelled to after escaping. These signs tell William Buckley's story.

"The Wild White Man"

One day, William saw a group of European settlers. He decided to greet them and give himself up, and he left the Wathaurong tribe.

When William came into their camp, he was dressed in animal furs. People must have been surprised at the way he looked! They called him "the Wild White Man".

A Free Man

In August 1835, William was given a **pardon** by the governor of Van Diemen's Land, Sir George Arthur. William was thanked for helping to keep the peace between the European settlers and the Aboriginal people. William was a free man!

A Pardon

A pardon set a convict free. There were two types of pardons:

- a conditional pardon – they were free, but were not allowed to go back to England.
- an absolute pardon – they were able to return to England, with no criminal record.

That's the time machine! It's time to go.

I really want to know what happened to William when he became a free man. But if I don't get back to the time machine, I'll never get home!

I'll go to the library when I get back to find out more about this "Wild White Man"!

William's New Life

I find out that in 1835, William moved to a settlement in the area that is now called Melbourne. He was among one of the two groups that began this new settlement.

He worked as an **interpreter** and peacekeeper between the European settlers and the Aboriginal people.

Melbourne, 1840

Batmania!

Melbourne was first known as Batmania and as Bearbrass! Batmania was after John Batman, a **founder** of Melbourne, and Bearbrass was probably after the Aboriginal name for the area, Berren or Bararing.

It was later renamed Melbourne, in March 1837, after Lord Melbourne, the Prime Minister of Great Britain.

William was quite unhappy with his new life in the settlement of Melbourne. He did not feel fully trusted by the European settlers or by the Aboriginal people. So he decided to leave Melbourne after only two years.

He settled in Van Diemen's Land, in Hobart Town, now known just as Hobart.

In Hobart Town, William had a number of jobs including a gatekeeper at a women's prison and a storekeeper at the Immigrants House.

Hobart Town, Van Diemen's Land

William lived in Van Diemen's Land for 19 years. In 1840, he was married to Julia Eagers. He died after falling from a horse and cart in 1856. He was 75 years old.

What an Interesting Life

William Buckley was the only known settler to have lived with Aboriginal people for such a long time.

William Buckley's stories help give a better understanding of Aboriginal customs and the way the Aboriginal people lived for thousands of years.

Buckley's Chance!

The saying "Buckley's chance" means you have no chance. Some people believe this saying comes from the unlikely survival of William Buckley.

Indigenous Languages

Before European settlement, there were about 250 Australian Indigenous languages. Most Indigenous people could speak five or more languages each. That way, they could speak to others who lived nearby.

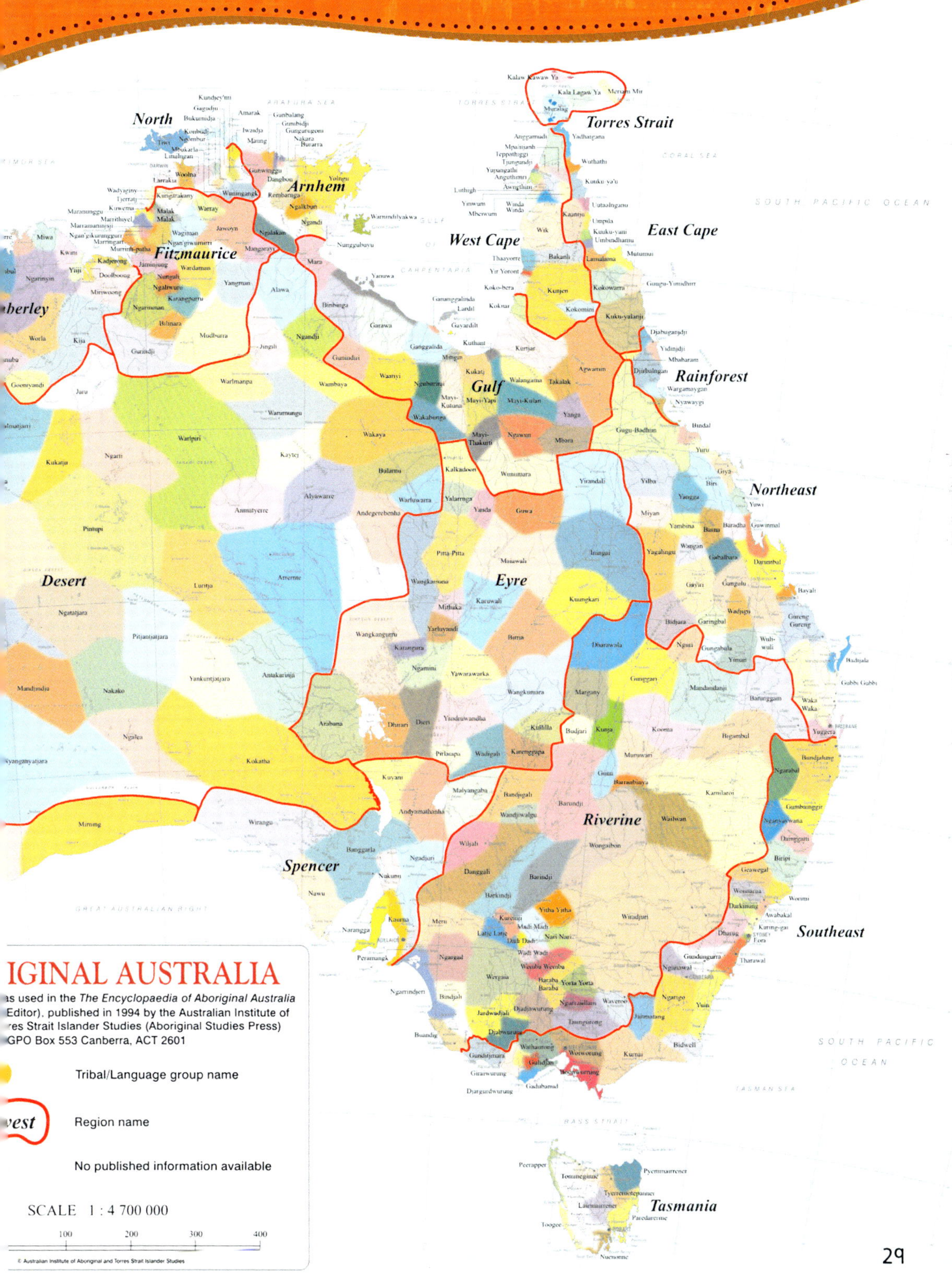
IGINAL AUSTRALIA
as used in the The Encyclopaedia of Aboriginal Australia
Editor), published in 1994 by the Australian Institute of
res Strait Islander Studies (Aboriginal Studies Press)
GPO Box 553 Canberra, ACT 2601
Tribal/Language group name
vest
Region name
No published information available
SCALE 1 : 4 700 000
100
200
300
400
© Australian Institute of Aboriginal and Torres Strait Islander Studies
North
Arnhem
Fitzmaurice
berley
Torres Strait
West Cape
East Cape
Rainforest
Gulf
Northeast
Desert
Eyre
Riverine
Spencer
Southeast
Tasmania
ARAFURA SEA
TORRES STRAIT
CORAL SEA
SOUTH PACIFIC OCEAN
GREAT AUSTRALIAN BIGHT
BASS STRAIT
TASMAN SEA
SOUTH PACIFIC
OCEAN
Kalaw Kawaw Ya
Kala Lagaw Ya
Meriam Mir
Yadhaigana
Wuthathi
Kuuku ya'u
Uutaalnganu
Umpila
Kuuku-yani
Umbindhamu
Lamalama
Kokowarra
Kunjen
Kokomini
Kuku-yalanji
Djabugandji
Yidindji
Mbabaram
Djirbalngan
Wargamaygan
Nyawaygi
Bindal
Yuru
Giya
Biri
Yuwi
Barna
Baradha
Guwinmal
Darumbal
Bayali
Gurang
Gureng
Gureng
Wuli-wuli
Badjala
Gubbi Gubbi
Waka Waka
Yuggera
Bundjalung
Gumbainggir
Ngarabal
Dainggati
Biripi
Geawegal
Worimi
Awabakal
Darkinung
Dharug
Tharawal
Gundungurra
Ngunawal
Yuin
Bidwell
Kurnai
Jaitmatang
Waveroo
Taungurong
Woiwurung
Boonwurrung
Gadubanud
Djargurdwurung
Girai wurung
Gunditjmara
Bunandig
Bindjali
Jardwadjali
Djadjawurung
Wergaia
Ngargad
Wemba Wemba
Wadi Wadi
Nari Nari
Madi Madi
Ladji Ladji
Dadi Dadi
Yitha Yitha
Barkindji
Barindji
Danggali
Wiljali
Wiradjuri
Wongaibon
Wailwan
Kamilaroi
Barundji
Bandjigali
Wandjiwalgu
Malyangaba
Pirlatapa
Wadigali
Karenggapa
Kullilla
Budjari
Kunja
Muruwari
Gwamu
Bigambul
Kooma
Mandandanji
Barunggam
Gunggari
Margany
Dharawala
Bidjara
Ngatu
Gungabula
Yiman
Garingbal
Wadjigu
Gangulu
Gayiri
Kuungkari
Iningai
Yagalingu
Wangan
Gabalbara
Yambina
Miyan
Yilba
Yirandali
Yangga
Gugu-Badhun
Mbara
Ngawun
Yanga
Takalak
Agwamin
Walangama
Mayi-Yapi
Mayi-Kulan
Mayi-Kutuna
Mayi-Thakurti
Wakabunga
Ngaburana
Kukatj
Kurtjar
Kuthant
Gayardilt
Lardil
Kokatj
Koko-bera
Yir Yoront
Thaayorre
Bakanh
Wik
Kaantju
Winda Winda
Mbewum
Yinwum
Luthigh
Awngthim
Anguthimri
Yupangathi
Tjungundji
Teppathiggi
Mpalitjanh
Anggamudi
Muralag
Gkalkbun
Ngandi
Nunggubuyu
Warnindilyakwa
Yolngu
Dangbon
Rembarnga
Gunwinggu
Wuningangk
Woolna
Larrakia
Ngalakan
Mangarayi
Mara
Yanyuwa
Alawa
Binbinga
Garawa
Gananggalinda
Ganggalida
Gunindiri
Nganji
Waanyi
Wambaya
Warumungu
Jingili
Mudburra
Warlmanpa
Wakaya
Bularnu
Kalkadoon
Wanamara
Yalarnga
Yanda
Guwa
Warluwarra
Andegerebenha
Alyawarre
Anmatyerre
Kaytej
Warlpiri
Ngarti
Kukatja
Pintupi
Luritja
Arrernte
Pitta Pitta
Maiawali
Wangkamana
Mithaka
Karuwali
Yarluyandi
Wangkangurru
Karangura
Ngamini
Yawarawarka
Wangkumara
Yandruwandha
Dieri
Dhirari
Arabana
Kuyani
Andyamathanha
Wirangu
Mirning
Kokatha
Ngalea
Nakako
Mandjindja
Ngaatjatjarra
Pitjantjatjara
Yankuntjatjara
Antakarinja
Barngarla
Ngadjuri
Nukunu
Nawu
Kaurna
Meru
Narangga
Peramangk
Ngarrindjeri
Jaru
Gooniyandi
Worla
Kija
Guriadji
Miwa
Kwini
Yiiji
Ngarinyin
Miriwoong
Doolboong
Kadjerong
Wadyiginy
Tjerraty
Kuwema
Maranunggu
Marrithiyel
Marramaninjsji
Ngan'gikurunggurr
Marringarr
Murrinh-patha
Jaminjung
Nungali
Ngaliwuru
Ngarinman
Karangpurru
Bilinara
Wardaman
Yangman
Wagiman
Jawoyn
Warray
Malak Malak
Kungarakany
Tiwi
Iwaidja
Maung
Amarak
Gunbalang
Gunbidji
Gungurugoni
Nakara
Burarra
Kundjey'mi
Gagudju
Bukurnidja
Peerapper
Tommeginne
Pyemmairrener
Tyerrernotepanner
Lairmairrener
Paredarerme
Toogee
Nuenonne

Buckley's Timeline

1780
Born in England

1795
Became a bricklayer's apprentice

1799
Became a soldier

8 May 1802
Found guilty of having stolen goods

27 April 1803
Transported to Australia

9 October 1803
Arrived in Australia at the Sullivan Bay penal settlement

December 1803
Escaped the penal settlement

Early 1804
Met the Wathaurong tribe

Joined John Batman's camp at Indented Head

6 July 1835

Left Melbourne to settle in Hobart Town, Van Diemen's Land

December 1837

Retired from work

1850

25 August 1835

Received a pardon from the governor

1840

Married Julia Eagers

2 February 1856

Died

Glossary

convicts people convicted (found guilty) of a crime

customs ways of doing things

European a person from Europe

founder someone who starts something

interpreter someone who helps people who speak different languages to understand each other

pardon to release from punishment; set free

penal settlement a place where convicts were kept

settlers people who move to another country to live, often to start a new colony

transported sent to live as a prisoner in another country

tribe a group of people living together, often related

Index